101 WAYS TO KNOW IF YOUR CAT IS ITALIAN

How to Talk To Your Cat About Their Secret
Life and the Essentials of Being Italian, A
Funny Cat Book and the Perfect Gift for Cat
Lovers and Those Who Love Italy

Seamus Mullarkey

101 Ways To Know If Your Cat Is Italian

Copyright © 2023 by Seamus Mullarkey

All rights reserved.

Plain Scribes Press

www.plainscribespress.com

DON'T MISS THIS SPECIAL BONUS

GET YOUR FREE BOOK TODAY...

IT'S SO SIMPLE – AND TOTALLY FREE!
– SCAN THE CODE OR CLICK THE LINK....

subscribepage.io/7565d5

Italy

INTRODUCTION

As a pet owner, you may think you know everything there is to know about your feline friend. But what if I told you that your cat has been keeping a secret from you all this time? What if I told you that your furry companion is actually Italian? That's right, your kitty may have been hiding their heritage from you all along!

Now, you may be wondering how you can approach this topic with your beloved pet. But fear not, for there are plenty of funny icebreakers that will get the conversation started. You could ask if they prefer traditional Italian pizza or the American version with a thick crust. You could inquire about their opinion on the best type of Italian wine or ask if they have a favorite Italian painter.

However, the real question you may be asking yourself is why your cat would keep their Italian heritage a secret. Perhaps they wanted to keep their cultural identity a mystery to seem more intriguing.

Regardless of the reason behind their secrecy, it's time to embrace your cat's true identity and celebrate its Italian heritage. You could plan a trip to Venice where you can explore the winding canals and indulge in some authentic Italian gelato together. Or, if your budget doesn't stretch to overseas jaunts with your kitty you could watch classic

Italian films like "La Dolce Vita" or "The Godfather" while sharing some prosciutto with your furry friend.

And let's not forget about the countless contributions that Italy has made to the world. Your cat could regale you with stories about famous Italian painters like Leonardo da Vinci or Michelangelo or tell you about the rich history of Rome and its iconic landmarks like the Colosseum or the Pantheon.

So go ahead, start a conversation with your Italian cat and uncover all the hidden gems of their heritage. Who knows, you may even discover a newfound love for all things Italian! The letter on the next page is an example of how you could get the conversation started about your cat and its heritage...

DEAR BELOVED FELINE COMPANION
– **MIO CARO GATTINO,**

I recently stumbled upon a revelation that I feel I must share with you. While sorting through your documents (strictly for tax purposes, mind you), I discovered that you are actually Italian!!

It all makes sense now. Your exquisite taste in cuisine, your delightful purrs that sound like a sweet serenade, and your penchant for soaking up the sun all hint at your Italian heritage. However, I must admit that I am perplexed as to how you managed to keep your lineage a secret from me for so long. Did you spend your time mastering the art of making pasta or perfecting your Italian accent when I wasn't around? Were you watching Fellini films while I was at work?

I'm so delighted to learn that you are Italian. Perhaps we could share some tasty treats while listening to Andrea Bocelli, or watch classic Italian films while lounging in the warmth of the sun. I would even be willing to consider a trip to Rome if it means experiencing Italy through your unique perspective.

While I may never be able to meow like an Italian, I am excited to learn more about your culture and language. Who knows, maybe you could teach me a few Italian phrases so that we can have even more meaningful conversations.

As they say in Itlay 'Mille bacci amore mio!!"

Your devoted human companion,

xxxxx

1

It bundles itself under the
blankets like a cannoli.

2

It's been laying on its cat tower so much, it resembles The Leaning Tower of Pisa.

3

It purrs when you call it
"bellissimo."

4

It loves relaxing to the soothing sounds of Frank Sinatra.

5

It can't help moving its paws around when it's telling a story.

6

Its tail flicks around like a long linguini.

7

If you upset it, you upset all its friends.

8

It wants to go shopping for a designer collar in Milan.

9

It doesn't like Italian
stereotypes but still watches
"The Sopranos."

10

It gets sad when you use tomato sauce in a jar from the store instead of making it yourself...

11

Those neighbors and their noisy
dogs give it '*agita*.'

12

It gives you this look if you eat dinner at a fake Italian restaurant like 'The Olive Garden.'

13

It knows all its family, even
the most distant cousins...

14

It wants to know "is the scungili fresh?"

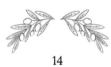

15

It loves its mama.

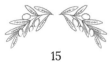

16

It wants to play 'bocce'
with its friends.

17

It believes in the *Dolce Far Niente*, the sweetness of sometimes doing nothing at all.

18

It demands the finest cat treats
— you know what Italians are
like about their food!

19

It likes to hang out with its 'amici'
on a warm summer evening.

20

It knows how to pose like Michelangelo's Statue of David.

21

When it's angry it snarls like
Joe Pesci — "you're dead, you
hear me! You're dead!"

22

It's Nonna's favorite!

23

It hates people being cheap:
"What? You only gave the
pizza guy a dollar?!"

24

Like *The Godfather*, it doesn't negotiate, it makes offers you can't refuse...

25

It'll stand on line for hours to get tickets to Ariana Grande or Madonna.

26

It curls up like 'maccheroni' when it naps.

27

It knocks everything off the table
except pictures of the pope.

28

Because mealtimes are important, it insists on nice dishes and glassware.

29

It's naturally stylish and knows all about *'la bella figura.'*

30

It wants its wet food to be shaped into meatballs.

31

It likes to keep up with news from the old neighborhood.

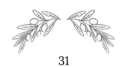

32

It gets like this when you bring home *frozen calzone* for dinner.

33

It knows the right sunglasses and jewelry make anybody look great.

34

It's impressed that you grow
your own basil.

35

It believes in handing down traditions to the next generation.

36

It always has lots of
family over for Sunday
dinner.

37

When it looks like this it's probably thinking of quotes from Dante's beautiful Italian poetry.

38

Like most cats it dislikes water, but it would be up for a gondola ride in Venice.

39

It has that one friend that always needs to be kept out of trouble.

40

It has one of those faces that remind you of an old Italian clown.

41

It dreams of visiting an old-style market in Little Italy.

42

It's loyal and is always there for you...

43

All its cat friends have nicknames like Tony Big-Ears or Tommy The Tail.

44

It will always protect its family.

45

It wants to live in a home as beautiful as an Italian palazzo.

46

It feels especially proud when it sees that green, white, and red.

47

Sometimes it looks like Al Pacino.

48

It flirts like Sophia Loren.

49

It wants to send a ball flying out of the park like Joe DiMaggio.

50

It looks forward to the
procession on its patron
saint's feast day.

51

It purrs like a Ducati motorcycle.

52

It likes to hear stories about 'la bella Italia.'

53

It scowls when it hears the name, "Al Capone": nothing like a crazy *pazzo* to give Italians a bad name.

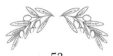

54

It's very particular about what toppings can go on the pizza Pineapple - Ugh!!

55

It gives great fashion advice and helps you look your best.

56

It's shocked if you
drink cappuccino after
breakfast.

57

It wants to run through the vineyards of Tuscany.

58

Its name ends with a vowel.

59

If you're a friend of a friend, it already considers you a part of the family.

60

It insists on being serenaded by
Pavarotti before bedtime.

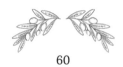

61

It likes all its food to be fresh as can be....

62

It starts out friendly - until you try to mess with it...

63

It kneads blankets and pillows as if they are pizza dough.

64

If it weren't a carnivore, this would be its carb of choice:

65

Like other clever Italians such as Leonardo da Vinci, it will discover a solution to any problem!

66

It makes friends wherever it goes.

67

It can be found cruising
around on a Vespa.

68

When it hears "let's play ball" it thinks of soccer.

69

It's not shy about giving hugs
and kisses.

70

Its toes are like cannellini beans.

71

It dreams of dancing the tarantella at an Italian wedding!

72

It doesn't like to leave the house looking scruffy - 'hey, mind the hair!'

73

It acts so crazy you think it's
been tasting the 'vino.'

74

It has an affinity for boot-shaped items.

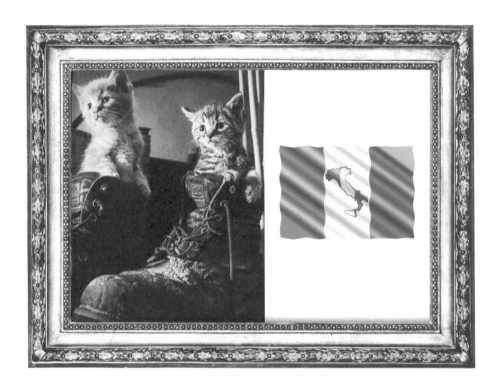

75

It looks so sad when
it hears songs about
"Bella Napoli."

76

It knows they break wine glasses at Italian weddings so it can't understand why you get so 'pazzo' about one little cup.

77

It looks exhausted the day after Columbus Day...

78

It wants a cat bed as big as the Colosseum in Rome.

79

It dreams of long summer days in Italy.

80

It perks up when it hears the clink of espresso cups.

81

It dreams of climbing to the top of Mount Vesuvius.

82

It knows how to live in the moment.

83

It stalks around the house
with the dramatic intensity of
an Italian opera.

84

It has an unspoken agreement of respect with other cats.

85

It values friendship and takes the
time to hang out with its *amici*.

86

It reminds you when it's time for an *aperitivo*.

87

At times it acts like Julius Caesar ruling an empire.

88

It gets argumentative about how long the pasta should cook.

89

It zips around faster than a brand-new Ferrari.

90

It takes offense when you serve it cheap cat food. You know how particular Italians are about their food...

91

It's the cutest little 'bambino' you've ever seen.

92

It wants to scamper around the cobblestone streets of Florence.

93

It likes to work on its tan.

94

It likes to dress up nice for formal occasions — "*che bello!*"

95

Its heart breaks at the sound of spaghetti being snapped in half.

96

It guards the *melanzane* in Nonno's vegetable garden.

97

It relaxes with a little 'riposo' whenever it can.

98

It loves licking the froth from an extra-milky 'caffè latte.'

99

Even if it lives in its parents' basement, it looks like it belongs in a penthouse.

100

It greets all the neighborhood cats
with a friendly *'buongiorno.'*

101

It has the sweetest way of saying "arrivederci!"

Now, all these Italian cats are worn out and gotta' take a nap.... *Ciao!!*

Goodbye from the cats of Italy...

CONCLUSION

And there you have it, amici - 101 Ways to Know if your Cat is Italian. We hope you've enjoyed this tongue-in-cheek guide to whether your kitty has Italian heritage or not.

From their love of basking in the sun to their refined palate for Italian cuisine, you may have found out that your furry feline friend has more in common with their Italian counterparts than you ever could have imagined.

So next time your cat starts meowing like they're from the old country, or they insist on being fed prosciutto with their kibble, you'll know why. And who knows, maybe you'll even start learning Italian together so you can communicate with each other in a whole new way...

By the way, if you're looking to start a conversation with your Italian cat, there are plenty of fun icebreakers to get things rolling. You could ask if they prefer Parmesan or mozzarella on their pizza, or inquire about their favorite Italian opera. Perhaps you could bring up the topic of spaghetti, or ask if they know any good Italian proverbs. And of course, you could always try meowing in an Italian accent to see if they respond.

Again, *mille grazie* for joining us on this whimsical journey of feline discovery. May you and your furry friend continue to enjoy all the joys that come with being an honorary Italian cat.

Ciao!

DON'T MISS THIS SPECIAL BONUS

GET YOUR FREE BOOK TODAY...

IT'S SO SIMPLE – AND TOTALLY FREE!
– SCAN THE CODE OR CLICK THE LINK....

subscribepage.io/7565d5

Please leave a review...

If this book brought you a few moments of pleasure, I'd be so grateful if you took just a few moments to leave a review on the book's Amazon page.

You can get to the review page simply by following the link

or QR code below. Thanks!

Purrr-leeze leave a review!

About the Author

A cat fanatic and book lover, I write fascinating books about our beloved kitties and how they've shaped our world.

— If you love cats, you'll love my books —

So, why not join my "Cats of the World" fan club? You can read all my new books FOR FREE?

AND... You'll get a free bonus book, "How to Speak French With Your Cat"...

SIMPLY SCAN THE CODE OR CLICK THE LINK TO JOIN!
There's no cost to you

subscribepage.io/7565d5

More from Seamus Mullarkey

Would you like to read more of my books???
Just click or scan below...

**SCAN TO VIEW
DETAILS...**

More from Seamus Mullarkey

Would you like to read more of my books???
Just click or scan below...

**SCAN TO VIEW
DETAILS...**

More from Seamus Mullarkey

Would you like to read more of my books???
Just click or scan below...

**SCAN TO VIEW
DETAILS...**

More from Seamus Mullarkey

Would you like to read more of my books???
Just click or scan below...

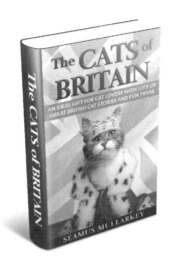

**SCAN TO VIEW
DETAILS...**

... and there's lots more to come ...

Scan the code or click the link so you get notified the minute I release a new book...

SCAN TO FOLLOW ME

Made in United States
Troutdale, OR
08/05/2024